A Different Kind of Christmas
Small Group Leader Guide

A DIFFERENT KIND OF CHRISTMAS: LIVING AND GIVING LIKE JESUS

An Advent Program by Mike Slaughter

Book: Christmas Is Not Your Birthday

In five short, engaging chapters, readers are inspired to approach Christmas differently and to be transformed in the process.
978-1-4267-2735-1

DVD With Leader Guide

Video programs about five to ten minutes each to accompany and complement the book, one video for each of the five chapters. Leader guide contains everything a leader needs to organize and run a five-session Advent study based on the book and videos, including discussion questions, activities, and flexible session lengths and formats.
978-1-4267-5354-1

Devotional Book: Devotions for the Season

Five weeks of devotional readings for program participants. Each reading includes Scripture, a brief story or meditation, and a prayer.
978-1-4267-5360-2

Youth Study Edition

A five-session Advent study for youth in support of the program. Written in a style and approach to inspire youth. Includes leader helps.
978-1-4267-5361-9

Children's Leader Guide

Complete lesson plans for a five-session Advent study for younger and older children, including activities and handouts.
978-1-4267-5362-6

Mike Slaughter's

A DIFFERENT KIND OF CHRISTMAS

Living and Giving Like Jesus

Small Group Leader Guide
by Ella Robinson

Abingdon Press
Nashville

Mike Slaughter's
A DIFFERENT KIND OF CHRISTMAS:
LIVING AND GIVING LIKE JESUS

Small Group Leader Guide by Ella Robinson

Copyright © 2012 by Abingdon Press
All rights reserved.

This book is printed on acid-free, elemental chlorine-free paper.

ISBN 978-1-4267-5363-3

12 13 14 15 16 17 18 19 20 21 — 10 9 8 7 6 5 4 3 2 1

MANUFACTURED IN THE UNITED STATES OF AMERICA

Contents

Introduction 7

1. Expect a Miracle 15

2. Giving Up on Perfect 25

3. Scandalous Love 35

4. Jesus' Wish List 43

5. By a Different Road 51

Organizing a Churchwide Program 61

Introduction

Christmas has been hijacked. Beginning in early October, we see holiday banners hanging from shopping mall ceilings and plastic trees lining store shelves. Christmas music begins to fill the airwaves as fall pumpkins are turning bright orange. Each year, the sights and sounds of Christmas come a little earlier, and merchandise gets a little more tempting.

This Advent study, *A Different Kind of Christmas: Living and Giving Like Jesus,* encourages us to move our focus away from consumerism and to reclaim the real meaning of Christmas, the birth of Jesus. Study participants will be inspired to establish new Christmas traditions that focus on Jesus Christ.

This study is part of a churchwide program that includes parallel five-week studies for adults, youth, and children, so your whole church family can participate in the effort to reclaim Christmas. (See Organizing a Churchwide Program, at the end of this leader guide.)

An important complement to the study is Mike Slaughter's devotional book, *A Different Kind of Christmas: Devotions for the Season.* You and your family will find daily joy and inspiration in Mike's devotions, which are themed to go with the study. Each devotion consists of a Scripture, a story from Mike's life and ministry, and a prayer.

THE STUDY

The adult study consists of three components:
- Mike Slaughter's book, *Christmas Is Not Your Birthday*;
- a DVD with videos for small group use;
- this leader guide.

Study participants will read one chapter of *Christmas Is Not Your Birthday* prior to each study session, and then meet together for group study each week for five weeks. During group study, participants will view a video presentation by Mike Slaughter and explore content from the book, video, and Bible, through discussion and activities.

Participants should have a copy of the book *Christmas Is Not Your Birthday* far enough in advance of the first session so they can read the Introduction and Chapter 1 and be prepared for group discussion. You may want to have extra copies of the book available at the first meeting so people who join the group at that time can take a copy home and use it to prepare for the next week's session.

Encourage group members to underline or highlight portions of each chapter as they read. Some of them may want to obtain a spiral-bound notebook or journal for this study so they can take notes about questions or points that they would like to make during the group sessions.

Assure participants who have already read *Christmas Is Not Your Birthday* that their participation in the study will enhance their understanding of the book; watching the video and participating in group discussions will give them a new learning experience and an opportunity for spiritual growth. Ask participants who have read the book before to read it again, one chapter per week, along with the other group members. Not only will this refresh their memory but it will also provide them with new insight and understanding.

How to Use This Leader Guide

A Quick Overview

As group leader, your role will be to facilitate the weekly sessions using this leader guide and the accompanying DVD. Because no two groups are alike, this guide has been designed to give you flexibility and choice in tailoring the sessions for your group. You may choose one of the following format options, or adapt these as you wish to meet the schedule and needs of your particular group. (Note: The times indicated within parentheses are merely estimates. You may move at a faster or slower pace, making adjustments as necessary to fit your schedule.)

Basic Option: 60 minutes

Opening Prayer	(2 minutes)
Biblical Foundation	(3 minutes)
Video Presentation	(15 minutes)

Group Discussion	(30 minutes)
Taking It Home	(5 minutes)
Closing Prayer	(< 5 minutes)

Extended Option: 90 minutes

Opening Prayer	(2 minutes)
Biblical Foundation	(3 minutes)
Opening Activity	(10–15 minutes)
Video Presentation	(15 minutes)
Group Discussion	(30 minutes)
Group Activity	(15 minutes)
Taking It Home	(5 minutes)
Closing Prayer	(< 5 minutes)

Although you are encouraged to adapt the sessions to meet your needs, you also are urged to make prayer and Scripture reading a regular part of the weekly group sessions. Feel free to use the opening and closing prayers provided here, or to create your own prayers. In either case, the intent is to "cover" the group session in prayer, acknowledging that only because of God's mercy and grace have we been forgiven of our sins. Scripture verses provided for each session are intended to serve as a biblical foundation for the group session, as well as for participants' continued reflection during the following week.

In addition to the session activities listed above, the following leader helps are provided to equip you for each group session:

- Fundamentals (materials to gather for the meeting)
- Key Insights (summary of main points from the week's content)
- Leader Background (additional information related to topic)
- Notable Quote (important quotation from the week's content)

You may use these leader helps for your personal preparation only, or you may choose to incorporate them into the group session in some way. For example, you might decide to review the key insights from the video either before or after group discussion, incorporate the leader extra into group discussion, or close the session with the notable quote.

At the end of the materials provided for each group session, you will find a reproducible participant handout. This handout includes key insights and "Taking It Home" application exercises for the coming week. Each week, you will have the opportunity to remind participants that these exercises are designed to help them get the most that they possibly can out of this study. They alone are the ones who will determine whether or not this is just another group study or a transformational experience that will have a lasting impact on their lives.

Helpful Hints

Here are a few hints that you may find useful for preparing and leading the weekly group sessions. Become familiar with the material before the group session. If possible, watch the DVD segment in advance.

- Choose the various activities to use during the group session, including the specific discussion questions you plan to cover. (Highlight these or put a checkmark beside them.) Remember, you do not have to use all the questions provided, and you can create your own.
- Secure a TV and DVD player in advance. Oversee room setup.
- Begin and end on time.
- Be enthusiastic. Remember, you set the tone for the class.
- Create a climate of participation, encouraging individuals to participate as they feel comfortable.
- Communicate the importance of group discussions and group exercises.
- To stimulate group discussion, consider reviewing the key insights first and then asking participants to tell what they consider to be highlights of the book and DVD segment.
- If no one answers at first, don't be afraid of a little silence. Count to seven silently; then say something such as "Would anyone like to go first?" If no one responds, venture an answer yourself. Then ask for comments and other responses.
- Model openness as you share with the group; group members will follow your example. If you share at a surface level, everyone else will follow suit.
- Draw out participants without asking them to share what they are unwilling to share. Make eye contact with someone and say something such as "How about someone else?"
- Encourage multiple answers or responses before moving on.
- Ask "Why?" or "Why do you believe that?" to help continue a discussion and give it greater depth.

- Affirm others' responses with comments such as "Great" or "Thanks" or "Good insight"—especially if this is the first time someone has spoken during the group session.
- Give everyone a chance to talk, but keep the conversation moving. Moderate the discussion to prevent a few individuals from doing all the talking.
- Monitor your own contributions. If you are doing most of the talking, back off so you do not train the group to keep quiet.
- Remember that you do not have all the answers. Your job is to keep the discussion going and encourage participation.
- Honor the time schedule. If a session is running longer than expected, get consensus from the group before continuing beyond the agreed-upon ending time.
- Consider involving group members in various aspects of the group session, such as asking for volunteers to run the DVD, read the prayers or say their own, read the Scripture, and so forth.

Above all, remember to pray. Pray for God to prepare and guide you, pray for your group members by name and for whatever God may do in their hearts and lives, and pray for God's presence before each group session. Prayer will both encourage and empower you for the weeks ahead.

Finally, if you are a first-time leader, remember that many characters in the Bible were hesitant and unsure of accepting God's call to lead, but God never abandoned any of them. Rest assured that God will be with you, too. After all, Jesus promised, "I am with you always, to the end of the age" (Matthew 28:20 NIV).

1. Expect a Miracle

PLANNING THE SESSION

Fundamentals
1. Confirm your meeting place and time.
2. Secure a TV and DVD player, and ensure that they are operational.
3. Obtain extra copies of *Christmas Is Not Your Birthday* to have on hand so that each participant will have a copy to use during the study session.
4. Have extra Bibles available for participants to use during the study session.
5. Obtain newspapers and magazines that participants can cut apart during a group activity.
6. Secure paper, pencils, scissors, and glue sticks or tape for participants to use during group activities.
7. If your meeting area has Internet access, secure one or more computers and the necessary information for connecting to the Internet.

Session Goals
This session is intended to help participants
- identify their mental picture of God;
- understand that their mental picture of God shapes their faith and values;
- realize how distorted Christians' view of Christmas has become;
- hear that the message of Christmas is about a sacrificial gift;
- understand that Christmas is the celebration of a miracle;
- realize that God's miracles are conceived and delivered through ordinary people who are willing to act on God's vision.

Key Insights
1. The picture that you have of God has everything to do with the shaping of your faith and values. If your picture of God is distorted, your life perspective will be skewed.
2. The real meaning of Christmas gets lost in shopping, spending, escalating debt, making exhausting preparations, and building stacks of gifts that are not needed or will not be used. In the chaos of the holiday season, we miss the true gift of Immanuel, God with us.
3. Debt driven by the spirit of materialism holds many Christians captive today. Jesus came to break the chains of oppression and bondage—even the chains of debt.
4. Debt creates incredible economic challenges for families. Slaughter says that in 2005, for the first time in U.S. history, Americans reached a negative savings rate. Americans were spending $1.22 for every $1 earned.

5. It's time for Christians to focus on Jesus' birthday and celebrate Christmas in a way that honors the birth of the Messiah—concentrating their resources on the least and the lost.
6. Every work of God is conceived in the heart of a disciple, grows in conviction and clarity of vision, and then is delivered through God's intended action; more simply stated, God births miracles through ordinary people.
7. Throughout Scripture, God chose ordinary, unqualified people through whom to perform miracles—Moses, David, Elizabeth, Mary, and others.
8. The power of Immanuel is the power to create change in the world through God's action in your life.
9. Grace may be free, but it is never cheap. Miracles come at a cost.

Leader Background

- Jesus spoke more about money and materialism than any other single topic except the kingdom of God.
- One definition of miracle describes it as "a visible interruption of the laws of nature, understood only by divine intervention and often accompanied by a miracle worker."
- Although Elizabeth and her husband, Zechariah, were devout believers, traditional thought was that a childless couple was not in God's favor. They faced scorn and ridicule from their neighbors.
- Under Old Testament law an unwed mother faced possible punishment by stoning.

GETTING STARTED

Opening Prayer

Merciful heavenly Father, as we begin this study of the celebration of the birth of your most precious miracle, open our eyes that we may see you clearly; open our ears that we may hear your voice; and open our heart that we may be a vessel for your use. We praise your name and lift our thanksgiving to you for the sacrificial gift of your son, Jesus. Bless this time of learning, sharing, and celebration. Amen.

Biblical Foundation

Therefore the Lord himself will give you a sign: The virgin will be with child and will give birth to a son, and will call him Immanuel (Isaiah 7:14 NIV).

Opening Activity

Choose one.

• Divide the group into two smaller groups. Set out newspapers and magazines that can be cut, glue sticks, tape, scissors, and blank paper. Instruct participants to work together with their small group and use the newspapers and magazines to make a collage. One group should make a collage showing the consumer's view of Christmas while the other group makes a collage of the Christian view of Christmas. When groups have finished with their collages, have them come back together and share their collages. Lead a discussion of how the real meaning of Christmas has gotten lost in the shopping mall.

• Ask the group to call out the many names for Jesus—Wonderful Counselor, Mighty God, Everlasting Father, Prince of Peace, Messiah King, and so forth. Write these names on a board as the group calls them out. Then give each participant a piece of paper and a pencil. Instruct them to review the names of Jesus that you have written on the board, and from those names create a drawing of what Jesus looks like. When everyone is finished, ask for volunteers to show their pictures and tell why they drew what they did.

LEARNING TOGETHER

Video Presentation
Play the DVD segments for Introduction and Session 1.
Running Times: 00:46 and 13:06

Group Discussion
In Session 1 of the book and video, "Expect a Miracle," Mike Slaughter points out that Jesus was not what most people expected. He did not possess worldly wealth or majestic power. In fact, he resisted the world's obsessions with wealth, pleasure, power, and recognition. In spite of this, we have allowed materialism and consumerism to skew our view of Jesus. We have created a Santa Claus Jesus who promises to fulfill all our earthly wants and wishes.

Ask participants to share how Christmas celebrations in their lives have changed throughout the years since they were children. This discussion may be especially interesting if you have a wide range of ages in your group. Then ask:

• If Jesus were a guest at your family's Christmas celebration, what would he observe? Would you change anything if you knew he was coming? Would you or your guests act differently?
• What are some things you currently enjoy or love about the holiday season? What don't you like? Is there a common theme between what you like and don't like?

Slaughter points out that the real meaning of Christmas is the celebration of a miracle—the birth of the Messiah. Jesus' mother, Mary, was an ordinary girl chosen to grow and deliver God's precious miracle. Today God still works miracles through ordinary people. God plants the seeds of miracles in the hearts of available people who are willing to act on God's vision.

Ask participants to imagine how Mary felt after speaking with the angel. Did she feel qualified for such an awesome responsibility? What did she do to prepare for delivering God's miracle? Ask:

• Why do you think God chooses to deliver miracles through ordinary people?
• How can we prepare to deliver the miracle that God is growing in our heart?

As Mary suffered the pains of childbirth in order to deliver God's miracle to Earth, we must suffer the pain of sacrifice if we are to deliver God's miracles to the world today. Most of us go to great extremes to avoid discomfort and sacrifice. When we do acknowledge pain and sacrifice, we tend to sanitize it. Ask the group:

• What do you think the author means by the statement

"Grace may be free, but it is never cheap? "
- Have you ever witnessed or experienced a miracle? If so, what happened?
- Do you think God could actually work a miracle through your life?
- What ideas do you have that could be seeds for a mission miracle? How could this group help to make it happen?

Group Activity
Choose one.
- Provide the group with hymnals or copies of familiar Christmas carols. Call their attention to the author's short description of "Away in the Manger" on page 11 of Christmas Is Not Your Birthday. Ask the group to find other Christmas carols and suggest how each offers a sanitized version of Jesus' birth.
- If your meeting place has Internet access, look up the Sudan Project begun by Ginghamsburg United Methodist Church (www.thesudanproject.org). Spend time learning about this project that has helped many people in Africa.

WRAPPING UP

Taking It Home
Explain that there are two resources available to help participants with personal application each week.

First, there is the Participant Handout. (See the handout for Session 1, below.) Briefly review the "Taking It Home" application exercises included on the handout. Encourage participants to complete the activities during the coming week.

Second, there is the accompanying book, *Christmas Is Not Your Birthday,* which expands on the material covered in the weekly video presentations. Encourage participants to read the first chapter this week as a follow-up to this group session, and possibly to read the second chapter in preparation for the next session. Encourage participants who have not ordered or purchased copies of the book to do so now.

Notable Quote

"I praise God all the time that He knew exactly when I would be ready to listen and am so thankful He let me be a part of His plan" (Therese Garison in *Christmas Is Not Your Birthday,* page 17).

Closing Prayer

Lord God, we celebrate you and the birth of your precious son, Jesus. This time of learning and sharing has made us so aware of "God with us." We are grateful for your Word and the opportunity to study about the miracles that you perform. As we continue our study in the weeks ahead, prepare our hearts to conceive and deliver your miracles, and our feet to act on your vision. Amen.

1. EXPECT A MIRACLE
PARTICIPANT HANDOUT

Therefore the Lord himself will give you a sign: The virgin
will be with child and will give birth to a son, and will call him
Immanuel. (Isaiah 7:14 NIV)

Key Insights

1. The picture that you have of God has everything to do with the shaping of your faith and values. If your picture of God is distorted, your life perspective will be skewed.
2. The real meaning of Christmas gets lost in shopping, spending, escalating debt, making exhausting preparations, and building stacks of gifts that are not needed or will not be used. In the chaos of the holiday season, we miss the true gift of Immanuel, God with us.
3. Debt driven by the spirit of materialism holds many Christians captive today. Jesus came to break the chains of oppression and bondage—even the chains of debt.
4. Debt creates incredible economic challenges for families. Slaughter says that in 2005 for the first time in U.S. history, Americans reached a negative savings rate. Americans were spending $1.22 for every $1 earned.
5. It's time for Christians to focus on Jesus' birthday and celebrate Christmas in a way that honors the birth of the Messiah—concentrating their resources on the least and the lost.
6. Every work of God is conceived in the heart of a disciple, grows in conviction and clarity of vision, and then is delivered through God's intended action; more simply stated, God births miracles through ordinary people.

7. Throughout Scripture, God chose ordinary, unqualified people through whom to do miracles—Moses, David, Elizabeth, Mary, and others.

8 The power of Immanuel is the power to create change in the world through God's action in your life.

9. Grace may be free, but it is never cheap. Miracles come at a cost.

Taking It Home

- List ways you can focus on the presence of Jesus rather than on the presents you expect to give and receive this Christmas.
- Are there other ways you can avoid consumerism this Christmas?
- Think of some ideas you've had recently. Could any of them be the seeds of miracles that God has planted? What actions could you take to deliver God's miracle?

2. Giving Up on Perfect

PLANNING THE SESSION

Fundamentals
1. Confirm your meeting place and time.
2. Secure a TV and DVD player and ensure that they are operational.
3. Obtain extra copies of *Christmas Is Not Your Birthday* to have on hand so that each participant will have a copy to use during the study session.
4. Have extra Bibles available for participants to use during the study session.
5. Obtain newspapers and news magazines that participants can cut apart for use in group activities.
6. Provide scissors and clear tape for participants to use in group activities.
7. Secure an easel or some other way of displaying the poster that participants will make during the opening activity.

Session Goals
This session is intended to help participants
    • understand that our attempts to create a perfect Christmas

take the focus away from the real meaning of Christmas—
to celebrate the birth of the Messiah;
- realize that although God loves us and we are highly fa-
vored, we will still experience persecution, pain, and
suffering;
- keep in mind that, for many people, the Christmas season
is a reminder of painful life challenges;
- understand that the miracle of Jesus' birth came amidst
uncertainty, fear, and suffering;
- realize that we often experience the loving presence of
God in the midst of pain and suffering.

Key Insights
1. In our attempts to create the perfect Christmas, we overextend
ourselves emotionally, physically, financially, and relationally.
2. The Christmas season, for many, is a reminder of painful
life challenges: divorce, death of a loved one, job loss, and
other challenges.
3. Christmas is God's vivid reminder that amid the uncertainty,
God shows up to bring peace, purpose, joy, hope, and
wholeness.
4. Our Christmas traditions have sanitized Jesus' birth narrative by removing the event from its biblical and historical
context.
5. It is human nature to experience doubt.
6. God is always with us, even in the midst of our struggles.
7. God never intended for us to handle life's unexpected turns
by ourselves.
8. God often speaks to us through others who have experienced
similar struggles and have come out on the other side.

9. God can use our painful experiences as the seeds of hope for someone else's miracle.

Leader Background

- Jesus was born in a stable where animals were kept. The odor of animals would have brought flies and other insects. Mice, rats, and snakes probably lived in the stable where the animals' food was stored.
- Jesus spent his earliest years as a refugee in Africa escaping the genocide that Herod was committing in Judea against children aged two and under.
- God's favor does not come to us because of what we do or don't do. God favors his children unconditionally.
- Scholars believe Mary was between twelve and fifteen years old when she gave birth to Jesus.
- God's blessings to Mary also brought pain throughout her life—all the way to the foot of the cross.
- Many Christians struggle with doubt, even Mother Teresa. She often wrote about her "darkness of faith."

GETTING STARTED

Opening Prayer

Lord God, thank you for this time of learning and sharing. We're grateful for your Word and the ability to read and study about you and your mercy. Help us to process the insights we will learn today and use them as we prepare to celebrate the Christmas season. Amen.

Biblical Foundation

The angel said to her, "Do not be afraid, Mary, for you have found favor with God. And now, you will conceive in your womb and bear a son, and you will name him Jesus. Mary said to the angel, "How can this be, since I am a virgin?" (Luke 1:30-31, 34 NRSV).

Opening Activity

Choose one.

• The author points out that our Christmas traditions have sanitized Jesus' birth narrative by removing the event from its biblical and historical context. Give the group a few minutes to read through the section "A Sanitized Nativity" on pages 21-24, then lead participants to discuss: In what ways have we made the story of Jesus' birth, life, and death easier to cope with? Why do you think this has happened?

• Provide a stack of newspapers and news magazines that the participants can cut apart. Have the group look through the newspapers and magazines for stories about people in need. Ask them to cut out the stories and tape them to the poster board. At the end of this activity, place the poster on an easel and let it stand at the front of the meeting room throughout the group study.

LEARNING TOGETHER

Video Presentation

Play the DVD segment for Session 2.
Running Time: 13:17

Group Discussion

In the first chapter of Luke we learn that two cousins, both in exceptional circumstances, were going to have babies. Elizabeth was very old and had been married for many years, yet she had no children; Mary, on the other hand, was a teenager betrothed—not married—to a young man named Joseph. Ask the group to review the first chapter of Luke and discuss:

- How differently did Zechariah (Elizabeth's husband) and Mary respond to the angels who gave them news about the forthcoming birth of their sons?
- Why did the angels tell both Zechariah and Mary, "Do not be afraid"?
- What emotional and social pressures do you think the four people—Elizabeth and Zechariah, Mary and Joseph— might have felt in the months and days leading up to the birth of their sons?

Mike Slaughter points out that God's love for us doesn't mean that our paths will be neat and predictable. Bad things happen to good people. We would expect the coming of the Messiah to have been the perfect event; but, in fact, he was born to an unwed mother, in a stable where animal noises and smells were plentiful, during a time of political oppression and genocide. Walking in the way of Jesus is neither safe nor predictable. Ask the group:

- How was the reality of Jesus' birth different from Christmas stories we have heard? What can we learn from these differences?
- What are some examples from your own life or the lives of your friends of when God was with you during difficult times?

Group Activity
Choose one.

- Divide the group into two smaller groups—women in one group and men in the other. Ask the groups to discuss how they would have handled the situation as Mary (for the group of women) or Joseph (for the group of men). After an appropriate amount of time, have the groups come back together and share their ideas. (Note: if you have only men or women in your group, ask one group to discuss how they would have handled the situation as Mary or Joseph, and the other group to discuss how they would have handled the situation as Mary or Joseph's parents.)

- Ask a volunteer from the group to read aloud 2 Corinthians 11:23-30. Then lead in a discussion of why God would allow Paul to experience such persecution and suffering. End this activity by going over the news stories that participants taped to the poster board during the opening session. Ask the group to say sentence prayers based on one or more of the stories mentioned.

WRAPPING UP

Taking It Home
Remind the group that there are two resources available to help participants with personal application each week.

First, there is the Participant Handout. Briefly review the "Taking It Home" application exercises included in this week's handout (below). Encourage participants to complete the activities during the coming week.

Second, ask participants to read the second chapter this week as a follow-up to this group session, or the third chapter this week in preparation for the next group session. Encourage participants who have not ordered or purchased copies of the book to do so now.

Notable Quote
"God uses our painful experiences to become the seed of hope for someone else's miracle" (*Christmas Is Not Your Birthday,* page 35).

Closing Prayer
Lord, thank you for being with us during this session as we studied your word and work. We praise you for using imperfect people to carry out your perfect miracles. Go with us as we adjourn our meeting, and guide us in the week ahead as we celebrate the birth of your precious Son. Amen.

2. GIVING UP ON PERFECT PARTICIPANT HANDOUT

The angel said to her, "Do not be afraid, Mary, for you have found favor with God. And now, you will conceive in your womb and bear a son, and you will name him Jesus. Mary said to the angel, "How can this be, since I am a virgin?" (Luke 1:30-31, 34 NRSV)

Key Insights

1. In our attempts to create the perfect Christmas, we overextend ourselves emotionally, physically, financially, and relationally.
2. The Christmas season, for many, is a reminder of painful life challenges: divorce, death of a loved one, job loss, and other challenges.
3. Christmas is God's vivid reminder that amid the uncertainty, God shows up to bring peace, purpose, joy, hope, and wholeness.
4. Our Christmas traditions have sanitized Jesus' birth narrative by removing the event from its biblical and historical context.
5. It is human nature to experience doubt.
6. God is always with us, even in the midst of our struggles.
7. God never intended for us to handle life's unexpected turns by ourselves.
8. God often speaks to us through others who have experienced similar struggles and have come out on the other side.
9. God can use our painful experiences as the seeds of hope for someone else's miracle.

Taking It Home

- Think about what would make a perfect Christmas for you. What life challenges will you face this year that could affect your ability to celebrate Christmas fully?
- Do you know others who will be facing life challenges during the holiday season this year? How can you help them to celebrate Jesus' birth?

3. Scandalous Love

PLANNING THE SESSION

Fundamentals
1. Confirm your meeting place and time.
2. Secure a TV and DVD player, and ensure that they are operational.
3. Obtain extra copies of *Christmas Is Not Your Birthday* to have on hand so that each participant will have a copy to use during the study session.
4. Have extra Bibles available for participants to use during the study session.
5. Provide paper and pens or pencils for each participant to use in group activities.

Session Goals
This session is intended to help participants
   • understand that the incarnation is the revelation of God's scandalous love affair with humanity;
   • learn that no matter how much we focus on the secular celebration of Christmas, God is persistent in striving to bring us back to him;

- realize that God loves us and wants us even while we are under the influence of greed, selfishness, addiction, and deceit;
- Understand that God wants us to return his love by extending unconditional love to those in need.

Key Insights

1. The layers of emotional defenses we develop to protect ourselves in relating with others can carry over into our relationship with God.
2. Grace, God's scandalous love for us, is what Christmas is all about.
3. All of us are needy when it comes to God's scandalous love. We all need God's mercy and grace.
4. We have been created to find life and meaning through exclusive devotion to God, but many times we search for life's meaning in greed and materialism.
5. Even when we are derailed and lose our God-bearings, God is with us, offering scandalous love despite our failures.
6. Listening to the negativity of others, instead of to the encouraging voice of God, can squelch miracles that are about to happen.

Leader Background

- Hosea was deeply in love with his wife, although she was unfaithful to him. The prophet's experience is compared to God's experience with Israel. God loved Israel and gave them many gifts, which they readily accepted, but Israel rejected God in favor of idols.

- Hosea 14:4-5, expressing God's boundless love for Israel, has been called one of the most eloquent passages of Scripture.
- David was a hero with many human failures. He seduced Bathsheba, had her husband killed, and was unresponsive to the destructive actions of his children, which led to the death of many people (2 Samuel 11; 13; 14; 24). Yet, he had a deep love for God. Although David was imperfect and sinned many times, God used him as a vessel for many miracles.

GETTING STARTED

Opening Prayer

Lord, heighten our senses as we study your word and work. Help us become keenly aware of your voice as you speak to us through our study. Help us to understand the meaning of "scandalous love," and show us how to offer that love to needy people around us. Amen.

Biblical Foundation

Then the LORD said to me, "Go and love your wife again, even though she commits adultery with another lover. This will illustrate that the LORD still loves Israel, even though the people have turned to other gods and love to worship them" (Hosea 3:1 NLT).

Opening Activity
Choose one.

- The author points out that the Bible is filled with testimonials of innumerable failures who "went from zeros to heroes" as they learned to live by faith, embracing God's grace. David is one example. Lead the group in a brief discussion of how David went from a zero to a hero. Then, ask the group to identify other Bible stories of men and women who grew in God's grace despite their failures.
- Remind the group that in spite of David's failures resulting from his relationship with Bathsheba, he was a man of courageous faith. Ask a volunteer from the group to read aloud Psalm 139:13-17. Then ask the group to work independently in writing their own psalm of praise to God.

LEARNING TOGETHER

Video Presentation
Play the DVD segment for Session 3.
Running Time: 15:21

Note: You may want to preview this video before showing the group, to check challenging content.

Group Discussion
In *Christmas Is Not Your Birthday,* Mike Slaughter writes that we compromise our most fundamental beliefs in order to

be accepted by other people. We take on false personality traits and create layers of emotional defenses to protect ourselves from rejection from others. Although we try to be something we are not, and sometimes seem to be successful, we can't fool God.

God knew all about Gomer, Hosea's wife, and about the sinful actions of the Israelites, but still did not give up on them. God maintained a scandalous love for them.

Slaughter points out that Mary, the mother of Jesus, had scandalous love for God. No matter what others in the community thought or said about her condition, Mary clung to the promise of God's never-ending love. She didn't focus on her own emotional state or what others might say; instead, she praised God and rejoiced in his magnificent gift.

Lead the group in discussing the author's meaning of *scandalous love*. What would it mean for us to love others "scandalously"? How would that be different from the safe, cautious ways we often show Christ's love in the world?

Group Activity
Choose one.
- Ask a volunteer from the group to read aloud Hosea 1:2. Then lead a discussion of why God told Hosea to marry Gomer.
- Lead the group in a discussion of how we tend to "sell ourselves" to other things instead of making God our number-one love. Ask: In your life, what set of priorities do you struggle with the most?

WRAPPING UP

Taking It Home

Remind the group that there are two resources available to help participants with personal application each week.

First, there is the Participant Handout. Briefly review the "Taking It Home" application exercises for this session (below). Encourage participants to complete the activities during the coming week.

Second, encourage participants to read the third chapter of *Christmas Is Not Your Birthday* this week as a follow-up to this group session, or read the fourth chapter as preparation for the next session. Encourage participants who have not ordered or purchased copies of the book to do so now.

Notable Quote

"Those who have messed up most respond with the greatest gratitude for God's relentless love" (*Christmas Is Not Your Birthday,* page 49).

Closing Prayer

Lord God, thank you for giving us your scandalous love, for not giving up on us even in the midst of our failures. Open our eyes and hearts, and allow us to see the people who are hurting and in need. Guide us in extending scandalous love to the people you place along our paths. Amen.

3. SCANDALOUS LOVE
PARTICIPANT HANDOUT

Then the LORD said to me, "Go and love your wife
again, even though she commits adultery with another
lover. This will illustrate that the LORD still loves Israel,
even though the people have turned to other gods and
love to worship them." (Hosea 3:1 NLT)

Key Insights
1. The layers of emotional defenses we develop to protect ourselves in relating with others carry over into our relationship with God.
2. Grace, God's scandalous love for us, is what Christmas is all about.
3. All of us are needy when it comes to God's scandalous love. We all need his mercy and grace.
4. We have been created to find life and meaning through exclusive devotion to God, but many times, we search for life's meaning in secular greed and materialism.
5. Even when we are derailed and lose our God-bearings, God is with us offering his scandalous love despite our failures.
6. Listening to the negativity of others instead of the encouraging voice of God causes miracles to be aborted.

Taking It Home
• Think about how your life might be different if you could fully understand and embrace God's passionate and unconditional love.

- When or where have you experienced God's relentless pursuit of you?
- How can you show "scandalous" love to others this holiday season because of God's great love shown to you?

4. Jesus' Wish List

PLANNING THE SESSION

Fundamentals

1. Confirm your meeting place and time.
2. Secure a TV and DVD player, and ensure that they are operational.
3. Obtain extra copies of *Christmas Is Not Your Birthday* to have on hand so that each participant will have a copy to use during the study session.
4. Have extra Bibles available for participants to use during the study session.
5. If your meeting area has Internet access, secure one or more computers and the necessary information for connecting to the Internet.
6. Provide paper and pens or pencils for each participant to use in group activities.

Session Goals

This session is intended to help participants
   • understand that Jesus wants us to give ourselves to him as a birthday present;

- understand that by serving others we are serving God;
- set new Christmas traditions that focus on Jesus, not on material goods.

Key Insights

1. We do not exist for ourselves; we exist to be the hands and feet of Jesus in the world. We are the only hands, feet, and wallets that Jesus has.
2. We serve God when we give our time, talents, and resources to meet others' needs in his name.
3. The more of ourselves that we give away, the more abundant our faith and contentment will be.
4. God creates miracles through the resources that we hold in our hands.
5. God sends us into the world to combat evil in Jesus' name.
6. At Christmas, we celebrate the sacrificial Messiah who was born to die for our sins. We too are called to give ourselves sacrificially for the world that God loves.
7. The word poverty is used in the Bible to indicate any kind of brokenness—personal or cultural—that restricts people from living in the fullness of humanity that God intends.

Leader Background

- In 1 John 3:16-18 we read that we are to lay down our lives for one another. When we see others in need, we are to show them love in action, not just talk.
- Christianity works not because we love God, but because God loved us by sending Jesus to atone for our sins (1 John 4:10).

- Only by obeying God and loving one another can Christians overcome the world (1 John 5:1-12).
- In 2004, Ginghamsburg United Methodist Church began a partnership with the United Methodist Committee on Relief and laid the foundation for the Sudan Project, a sustainable agriculture program in South Darfur. As a result:
  * More than 5,200 farming families were restocked with seed and supplies.
  * Programs for child protection and development have been implemented.
  * One hundred seventy-nine new schools have provided more than 22,000 children with safe havens and renewed hope.
  * Life-skills training centers equip young men and women with marketable trades.
  * Eighty-five thousand people have gained access to clean water.
  * As of mid-2011, over six million dollars have been invested in the Sudan Project by Ginghamsburg United Methodist Church alone (*Christmas Is Not Your Birthday,* page 65).

GETTING STARTED

Opening Prayer
Lord God, we thank you for allowing us to meet together and study your word. Erase the pressures of the day from our minds, and allow us to focus solely on your voice as you speak to us through today's study. In Jesus' name we pray, Amen.

Biblical Foundation

"The King will reply, 'I tell you the truth, whatever you did for one of the least of these brothers of mine, you did for me'" (Matthew 25:40).

Opening Activity

Choose one.

• Lead the group in discussing their Christmas traditions. Which ones are family traditions passed down through the years? Which are new traditions? Discuss how traditions become "traditions."

• Ask participants to work together as a group and search through Matthew, Mark, Luke, and John, looking for miracles performed by Jesus. Ask one person to be in charge of writing down the Bible reference and a brief description of the miracle. Conclude this activity by pointing out to the group that God creates miracles though the resources we hold in our hands. Moses' staff, David's five smooth stones, a lunch of five pieces of bread and two small fish—these are biblical examples of the resources from which miracles are made (*Christmas Is Not Your Birthday,* page 59).

LEARNING TOGETHER

Video Presentation

Play the DVD segment for Session 4.
Running Time: 15:54

Group Discussion

Mike Slaughter explains Kingdom Economics 101 in *Christmas Is Not Your Birthday*. He writes, "When we obediently release what is in our hands, Jesus blesses it, multiplies it, and then gives it back to us for the purpose of distribution." Moses' staff, David's five smooth stones, the widow's oil, six water jars at a wedding reception, another widow's two small coins, and a lunch of five pieces of bread and two small fish—these are resources that God used to make miracles. By obeying Jesus' directive to release what is in our own hands, we can save the lives of hundreds of thousands of people around the world.

During Jesus' earthly ministry, he told his followers they were responsible for feeding the hungry in their midst. Everyone who recognizes Jesus as Messiah is a servant of that same mission.Lead the group in a discussion of the Sudan Project. If your meeting place has Internet access, log on to the Web site (www.thesudanproject.org). Discuss how the project began and the accomplishments that are being achieved. How is the project's work possible?

Ask participants to turn to page 67 in *Christmas Is Not Your Birthday*. Have them read and discuss the testimony of the person who raised money for the Sudan project. Point out that not only did the group raise three thousand dollars for the project, but they also gained new members for their group. Discuss the concept of being the hands, feet, and wallets of Jesus.

Group Activity

Choose one.
- If you have Internet access at your meeting place, ask the group to work together and log on to the Web site for

Doctors Without Borders (www.doctorswithoutborders.org). Look through the site and note the health issues around the world that are described. Lead a discussion of how group participants could help others around the world.

• Lead the group in discussing what the following statement means: "We need to be committed to live more simply so that others may simply live." Ask the group to brainstorm ways in which they can live out this statement.

WRAPPING UP

Taking It Home

Remind the group that there are two resources available to help participants with personal application each week.

First, there is the Participant Handout. Briefly review the "Taking It Home" application exercises included in the handout for this session (below). Encourage participants to complete the activities during the coming week.

Second, ask participants to read the fourth chapter this week as a follow-up to this group session, or to read the fifth chapter in preparation for the next session. Encourage participants who have not ordered or purchased copies of the book to do so now.

Notable Quote

"We do not exist for ourselves; we exist to be the hands and feet of Jesus in the world" *(Christmas Is Not Your Birthday,* page 66).

Closing Prayer

Lord God, we thank you for sending your only son to sacrifice his life for us. What a wonderful gift you have given us. We thank you for your mercy and grace. Through Jesus you have given us eternal life with you. Lord, be with us as we adjourn our meeting today, and guide us to share your unending love with others in the coming week. Amen.

4. JESUS' WISH LIST
PARTICIPANT HANDOUT

The King will reply, 'I tell you the truth, whatever you did for one of the least of these brothers of mine, you did for me.' " (Matthew 25:40 NIV)

Key Insights
1. We do not exist for ourselves; we exist to be the hands and feet of Jesus in the world. We are the only hands, feet, and wallets that Jesus has.
2. We serve God when we give our time, talents, and resources to meet others' needs in his name.
3. The more of ourselves that we give away, the more abundant our faith and contentment will be.
4. God creates miracles through the resources that we hold in our hands.
5. God sends us into the world to combat evil in Jesus' name.
6. At Christmas, we celebrate the sacrificial Messiah who was born to die for our sins. We too are called to give ourselves sacrificially for the world that God loves.

Taking It Home
- Think about ways you can change the focus of your Christmas from self-indulgence to celebrating the birth of Jesus. What can you give Jesus on his birthday this year?
- How might you begin to give an equal amount of what you spend on yourself to a specific mission in your area or around the world? What missions will you consider?
- What traditions can you start this year to make every Christmas a more authentic celebration of Jesus' birth?

5. By a Different Road

Fundamentals

1. Confirm your meeting place and time.
2. Secure a TV and DVD player, and ensure that they are operational.
3. Obtain extra copies of *Christmas Is Not Your Birthday* to have on hand so that each participant will have a copy to use during the study session.
4. Have extra Bibles available for participants to use during the study session.
5. If you choose the craft activity, obtain coffee filters, paper towels, small cups, red food coloring, wooden skewers, scissors, green construction paper, and clear tape. Prepare one or more tables to be used for the craft time.

Session Goals

This session is intended to help participants

- understand the importance of allowing the lessons of Advent and Christmas to shape the way they start the New Year;

- become aware of ways they can commit to serve Jesus' mission for the least and the lost;
- develop an action plan for simplifying their outer space in order to open up inner space and release underused resources for God's mission.

Key Insights

1. With the beginning of the New Year, January is the traditional time to commit to taking a different road—to change the direction of our lives.
2. Simplifying our lifestyle reduces stress.
3. God's redemptive work in the world is multiplied when we give our treasures to Jesus.
4. Changing course—taking a different road—involves repentance.
5. Jesus spoke about money and possessions more than about any other topic—even more than prayer and faith combined.
6. Our outward world is a reflection of our inner world. When we clean up our outer space, we open up inner space and release underused resources for God's mission.
7. There are opportunities everywhere to be Christ's light by serving others' needs in practical ways.

Leader Background

- Epiphany is the celebration of the arrival of the wise men or "Magi" who came from afar to see the new King.
- Scholars estimate that it took about two years for the wise men to travel to see Jesus.

- Although many traditions assume that there were three Magi, the exact number is not known.
- The size of the American family has gotten smaller over the last thirty years, but our homes have gotten 42% larger *(Christmas Is Not Your Birthday,* page 77).

GETTING STARTED

Opening Prayer

Lord, guide us as we begin this week's study. Help us to set our focus on you and your desire for our lives. Show us the way so that we may follow you. Amen.

Biblical Foundation

On coming to the house, they saw the child with his mother Mary, and they bowed down and worshiped him. Then they opened their treasures and presented him with gifts of gold and of incense and of myrrh. And having been warned in a dream not to go back to Herod, they returned to their country by another route (Matthew 2:11-12 NIV).

Opening Activity

Choose one.

- The author begins this chapter with a personal reflection illustrating the principle that simplicity reduces stress. Ask for volunteers to share their own experiences with this principle. Follow up with a brainstorming session to

identify everyday ways to practice this principle.
• Make a coffee filter rose.

You will need:
- White coffee filters, enough for each participant to have one
- Small cups filled with two or three tablespoons of water, one cup for each participant
- One or more bottles of red food coloring
- Wooden skewers, one for each participant
- Clear tape
- Scissors
- Green construction paper
- Paper towels
- Disposable tablecloth

Place the craft supplies on a table large enough for all participants to sit around. (Use several tables if you have a very large group.) Cover the tabletop with a disposable tablecloth. Instruct participants to add three or four drops of food coloring to the water, then dip the coffee filter into the cup. They can remove the coffee filter quickly for a light pink color or leave it longer for a darker pink. Remove the coffee filter and squeeze the water out. Spread the filter on a paper towel to dry. Allow the filters to dry during the study session. Have participants leave the craft table and assemble for the group study.

LEARNING TOGETHER

Video Presentation
Play the DVD segment for Session 5.
Running Time: 12:34

Group Discussion
Epiphany is the celebration of the arrival of the wise men who traveled long distances to greet the Christ child. The story of these "Magi" is an inspiring example of persistent, life-altering faith. According to the information in the Gospel of Matthew, the Magi traveled for almost two years to reach the new King. They did not kneel at his manger but met with him in a house, perhaps one that the family had rented or the home of a family friend. Also, there is no definitive account of the number of wise men who visited Jesus, but by the sixth century people had decided on the number of Magi and had even named them.

Discuss how the true story of the wise men and their travels differs from the way we traditionally think of the Magi visiting the newborn Jesus. Why do you think we have changed the way we view the elements of the Christmas story?

Mike Slaughter points out that Jesus spoke about money and possessions more than any other topic. The way we spend money is a window to our true character; our bank statement is the truest measure of the current state of our faith. Ask for a volunteer to read Matthew 6:21. Then lead the group in a discussion of how overspending, debt, and attachment to material possessions hinder our ability to fully commit to following Jesus in sacrificial mission. Ask another volunteer to read the story of the man who had great wealth in Mark 10:17-22. Give the group a few minutes to reflect silently on these Bible verses and the current state of their faith.

When Jesus sent his disciples into the world (Matthew 10:9-10), he told them to travel light. He did not want them to become overburdened with too much "stuff" or to be focused on money. Today many Christians have lost their focus on Jesus by becoming preoccupied with material possessions and the building of financial wealth. The more we have, and the harder we must work to maintain it, the less time we have to develop relationships with those closest to our hearts, and the less time we have to serve Jesus' mission for the least and lost.

Lead the participants in a discussion of Slaughter's statement: "Our outward world is a reflection of our inner world; we have to clean up outer space to open up inner space as well as to release underused resources for God's mission."

Group Activity
Choose one.

- Lead participants in a discussion of ways to simplify their home in order to create more room for peace and righteousness, rather than more "stuff." Ask: What excess can you get rid of in your home to reflect more accurately where your priorities lie?
- If you chose the craft activity for the Opening Activity, ask participants to return to the craft table. Instruct them to fold their filter in half so they have a half circle. Fold it in half again, making a pie shape. Cut the point off of the filter about one inch up from the tip, making a ring

shape when unfolded. Unfold the filter and cut from the center to the outside of the circle, making one long strip. Trim away some of the strip at an angle, making a long narrow triangle. Begin wrapping the narrow end of the strip around the end of a skewer.

• When the shape is wound around itself, it will look like a rose. Use a piece of clear tape and wrap it around the bottom of the rose tightly. Cut a small strip of green construction paper, then wrap it around the bottom part of the rose and down onto the skewer. Secure with clear tape.

As participants complete their rose, lead them in a discussion of how the ordinary possessions we have can become like beautiful roses to people in need. Explain that, like the man in Luke 12:18-20, we are foolish to store up things for ourselves and disregard the needs of God's children.

WRAPPING UP

Taking It Home

Remind the group that there are two resources available to help participants with personal application each week.

First, there is the Participant Handout. Briefly review the "Taking It Home" application exercises included in the handout for this session (below). Encourage participants to complete the activities during the coming week.

Second, ask participants to read the fifth chapter this week as a follow-up to this group session. Encourage participants who have not ordered or purchased copies of the book to do so.

Notable Quote

"You can't live with one foot in the kingdom of God and the other in the kingdom of consumption" *(Christmas Is Not Your Birthday,* page 76).

Closing Prayer

Lord, as we complete our study of a Different Kind of Christmas, *we are focused on you. We are filled with the cele-bration of Jesus' birth. We are ready to walk a different road, to tell others about your scandalous love and amazing grace. Guide us as a group and as individuals, as we seek out the lost and lonely who are waiting for us to tell them about your loving grace. Father, use us as your vessels to work miracles in the coming year. Amen.*

5. By a Different Road
Participant Handout

*On coming to the house, they saw the child with his
mother Mary, and they bowed down and worshiped him.
Then they opened their treasures and presented him with
gifts of gold and of incense and of myrrh. And having
been warned in a dream not to go back to Herod, they
returned to their country by another route.*
(Matthew 2:11-12 NIV)

Key Insights

1. With the beginning of the New Year, January is the traditional time to commit to taking a different road—to change the direction of our lives.
2. Simplifying our lifestyle reduces stress.
3. God's redemptive work in the world is multiplied when we give our treasures to Jesus.
4. Changing course—taking a different road—involves repentance.
5. Jesus spoke about money and possessions more than about any other topic—even more than prayer and faith combined.
6. Our outward world is a reflection of our inner world. When we clean up our outer space, we open up inner space and release underused resources for God's mission.
7. There are opportunities everywhere to be Christ's light by serving others' needs in practical ways.

Taking It Home

- Think of ways you can change your priorities so that this year you will focus on Jesus more and yourself less.
- Take time to declutter your closets and give underused resources to people who could use them. Tell the people to whom you give these items about the good news of Jesus.
- Make a commitment to demonstrate your faith by participating in practical service this year. Then, take the necessary steps to become involved in the area of service that you have chosen.

Organizing a Churchwide Program

A Different Kind of Christmas: Living and Giving Like Jesus is a practical and inspirational study for the Advent season. Based on Mike Slaughter's popular book *Christmas Is Not Your Birthday,* this five-week program will empower your family and your church to reclaim the broader missional meaning of Jesus' birth and to experience a Christmas season with more peace and joy than any toy or gadget could ever bring.

A churchwide Advent program for all ages will help people come to a deeper understanding of what the Christmas story teaches us about Jesus Christ and about God's will for our lives. It will offer opportunities for learning, for intergenerational activities, and for reaching out to the community.

Resources for the Churchwide Program
Adults
> *Christmas Is Not Your Birthday*—Book
> *A Different Kind of Christmas: DVD With Leader Guide*—Videos
> *A Different Kind of Christmas: A Season of Devotions*—Devotional companion

Youth

A Different Kind of Christmas: Youth Study Edition

Children

A Different Kind of Christmas: Children's Leader Guide

Schedule Suggestions

Many churches have weeknight programs that include an evening meal, an intergenerational gathering time, and classes for children, youth, and adults. The following schedule illustrates one way to organize a weeknight program.

- 5:30 p.m.: Gather for a meal.
- 6:00 p.m.: Have an intergenerational gathering that introduces the subject and primary Scriptures for that evening's session. This time may include presentations, skits, music, and opening or closing prayers.
- 6:15 p.m.–8:45 p.m.: Gather in classes for children, youth, and adults.

You may choose to position this study as a Sunday school program. This approach would be similar to the weeknight schedule, except with a shorter class time (which is common for Sunday morning programs). The following schedule takes into account a shorter class time, which is the norm for Sunday morning programs.

- 10 minutes: Have an intergenerational gathering that is similar to the one described above.
- 45 minutes: Gather in classes for children, youth, and adults.

Choose a schedule that works best for your congregations and its existing Christian education programs.

Activity Suggestions
Birthday Party for Jesus
An all-church party would be a good kick-off or wrap-up event. Take the opportunity to collect items as gifts for a local organization. Items for young children would be especially appropriate. Possible ideas include: children's books for a hospital library, baby supplies for a shelter, or school supplies for an elementary school.

All-church Food Drive
Lesson 1 in the Children's Leader Guide has instructions for families to organize a food drive and invite the entire church to participate. The food drive would last all five weeks of the study.

Service Projects
In Lesson 4 of the Children's Leader Guide, children will brainstorm ideas for a class service project. This idea could be expanded to become a churchwide service project. Alternatively, each age group could plan a service project and invite the whole church to participate.